twenty-first century ireland

GW00771116

# Savvy

# and the Preaching

# of the Gospel

A response to Vincent Twomey's
*The End of Irish Catholicism?*

Desmond Fennell

*VERITAS*

*Published 2003 by*
Veritas Publications
7/8 Lower Abbey Street
Dublin 1
Ireland

Email: publications@veritas.ie
Website: www.veritas.ie

ISBN 185390 746 4

10 9 8 7 6 5 4 3 2 1

A catalogue for this book is available from the British Library.

*Veritas books are printed on paper made from the wood pulp of managed
forests. For every tree felled, at least one tree is planted, thereby renewing
natural resources.*

Design by Pierce Design
Printed by Betaprint Ltd

# Savvy and the Preaching of the Gospel[1]

Vincent Twomey's *The End of Irish Catholicism?* has examined the present crisis of the Catholic Church in Ireland and sketched a programme of renewal. I enthusiastically endorse this programme, centred on faith, theology, liturgy, celebration in all its forms, and administrative restructuring. I missed sufficient emphasis on intellectual mastery and awareness of the secular situation and the use of this to make the preaching of the Gospel more effective. I want to argue for equal emphasis on this aspect of the Church's activity.

Broadly understood, the preaching of the Gospel can be engaged in by all Christians and take a great variety of forms. In these pages, while I have all those forms in the back of my mind, I am thinking mainly of the delivery of the Gospel by means of words and other symbols. This embraces speaking from the altar, doing a radio interview, teaching a religion class, taking part in a talk-show, writing books, newspaper articles or pastoral letters, running web-sites or radio or television stations, and publishing books, videos, cds, magazines or newspapers.

In whatever form, and even when done in love of God and one's neighbour, preaching the Gospel is not in itself a virtuous

---

1.    My thanks to David Quinn for help with some of my research for this essay, but its contents are entirely mine.

activity, but an attempt to be that. It is an effort to realise a good, namely, *effective communication of the Gospel.* And as with all efforts at realising goodness, it depends for its success on knowledge of the environmental reality in which it occurs. Traditionally, we have called the possession and employment of such knowledge 'prudence'.

In English the meaning of this word which names the first of the cardinal virtues – the one without which no other virtue can be exercised – has decayed. We rediscover its true meaning only in its dictionary definitions and their etymologies; for example, *discretion* and its derivation from Latin words for sifting and discernment; or even better, *circumspection* and its transparent meaning of 'noting the environment, taking everything into account'. The German for prudence, *Klugheit,* comes nearer to retaining the original vigour of the word. It derives from the adjective *klug,* which my German dictionary renders as, among other things, 'astute, alert, sagacious, cunning, shrewd, clear-sighted, discerning, wise'.

It is with *Klugheit* in mind that the German philosopher Josef Pieper writes:

> The pre-eminence of prudence means that realisation of the good [say, 'communication of the Gospel'] presupposes knowledge of reality. He alone can do good who knows what things are like and what their situation is. The pre-eminence of prudence means that so-called 'good intention' and so-called 'meaning well' by no means suffice. Realisation of the good presupposes that our actions are appropriate to the real situation, that is, to the concrete realities which form the 'environment' of a concrete human action; and that we therefore take this concrete reality seriously, with clear-eyed objectivity.[2]

---

2.    *Prudence,* London, Faber and Faber, 1959.

'Savvy' seems an adequate rendering of the virtue that Pieper is talking about. It expresses more or less what Christ had in mind when he commanded his disciples to be 'wise as serpents' in whatever they would do or say. He was telling them not to be 'clueless', but to be very much 'clued in'.

## Reflecting the situation

In all effective evangelisation, whether carried out by ordinary Christians or by professional evangelisers, savvy, meaning 'alert knowledge of how things are and the use of this in action', plays a basic role. It enables the evangeliser, who must use words and other symbols, to choose such as reflect the secular situation, general and particular, that is shared by him with the recipients of his message. This reflection by him of the lived-in situation, shared and more or less known by his recipients, furthers acceptance of the Gospel in either of two ways. When the recipients are well-disposed, it evokes trust in the evangeliser, and consequently openness to his message's Gospel core. When the recipients are ill-disposed, it evokes respect for the evangeliser, and a consequent weakening of the preconceived intention to reject what he is saying and to urge others to do so.

## Clarifying the situation

Beyond this basic role which savvy plays in all effective evangelisation, there is a further role it can play if, rather than being merely instinctive and approximate, it is intellectually profound and exact. When the savvy of the evangelisers has this quality, their cannily chosen language not only reflects the secular situation; it also clarifies it – and does so to a much greater degree than the politically conditioned explanatory discourse that the situation exudes. Their profound and exact savvy performs this function even when, because of limited time or the limited cognitive interest of an audience, they reveal only, so to speak, the foreground of what they know. Always, from the profound and precise background of their knowledge, flows an informed understanding of the immediate and particular. And this, regardless of time available or of audience, enables them to supply coherence to the disjointed perceptions of most people, of whatever educational background, regarding the way things are.

As occurs with the mere reflection of the shared situation in the evangeliser's discourse, so, too, with this clarification of it: it furthers acceptance of the Gospel in either of two ways. When the recipients are well-disposed, it evokes gratitude towards the evangeliser as for a gift received, and consequently a greater trustful openness to his message's Gospel core. When the recipients are ill-disposed, it disconcerts them by its perceptible but unwelcome truth, reduces their public standing (if they have such) as definers of the situation, and consequently lessens their ability to offer confident opposition to the Church's teaching and to build support for this. (Even a superficial perusal of the Gospels shows that this is a very Christ-like manner of dealing with opponents of the Good News.)

## Towards a grasp of the present situation

The drift of my argument must by now be apparent. I believe that, in recovering from its present crisis, the Irish Catholic Church collectively – but in particular its professional evangelisers, and most particularly its top leadership – need to have and use profound and exact knowledge of the contemporary secular situation and of the Church's place in it.[3] The relevant situation embraces the Western world from San

3.    I am writing about the necessary use of such knowledge for the effective preaching of the Gospel in Ireland. But in view of the fact that the Irish Church is a large corporate entity engaged in many activities, such knowledge is obviously also essential for its successful management, including its determination of strategies and its allocation of resources.

Francisco and Vancouver to Stockholm, Warsaw and Palermo. It obtains, in a particular, Irish form, throughout our island. For my part, greatly daring, and as an appetiser to what an 'intellectually profound and exact awareness' might be, I continue with a meditation on the situation I have just delimited.

* * *

## The change of rules

In the course of her book *Promiscuities*, an American feminist writer Naomi Wolf tells of her childhood in San Francisco. Recalling a memory from 1970, she writes:

> There were whispered arguments between our parents while we watched TV – arguments about changing the rules, we gathered, that applied to all of us, the dads and moms as well as the kids.

When I heard it said in Dublin and in places on the Continent, in the 1970s and 80s, it was in the past tense: 'The rules have changed, you know'. It was said when some incident or some topic of conversation suggested it, and was accompanied by a laugh or a regretful sigh.

However casually uttered, it was a momentous statement, or rather, a statement recording a momentous event. It meant that those who are in charge – the rulers and the ethical preachers they endorse – have changed the rules of right, wrong and permitted behaviour for 'the dads and moms and the kids'; and the new rules are being generally observed, have operative force. But 'the rules' in that broad sense mean 'the civilisation'. A civilisation is, essentially, *a hierarchical set of rules derived from a hierarchy of values, which is subscribed to by rulers and ruled and lasts because it presents sense.* So, that casual, oft-repeated statement was indicating the end of the civilisation previously lived in – the civilisation we call 'Western' – and its replacement by an ad hoc collection of new rules, which might sooner or later be ordered into a new civilisation and sense.

It was a statement doubtless heard in Rome and in other cities of the Roman Empire in the 50s and 60s of the fourth century, as the new, state-supported Christian dispensation began to take permanent effect. And then, too, doubtless, it was accompanied by a laugh or a sigh. Many outward signs of Roman continuity still remained. The rulers and their propaganda did not say 'the old civilisation has ended and a new one has begun' or words to that effect. In view of the shocks the system was experiencing from internal conflicts and barbarian incursions, that shock would have been too much. But Christian spokesmen and writers were saying it in as many words; and it was what in fact was happening, as subsequent history would clearly show.

A civilisation can end, and its rules be replaced by new rules, as a result of conquest. This happened in Christian North Africa and Spain in the seventh and eighth centuries, as Islam became established and accepted there. But it can also happen when powerful rulers, *intent on the maintenance or increase of their power*, perceive that, to effect this, a change of the reigning ideology is required. Acting on this perception, they endorse a new body of preachers who seem suitable for the task. It was with the maintenance of the Roman Empire in mind that Emperor Constantine and his ministers took such action in the fourth century. And it was as a result of their action that the Christian rules of behaviour became and remained, until the middle of the twentieth century, the core of European or Western civilisation, at home and overseas. 'The core', because ethical elements inherited from Rome, as well as European aristocratic and middle-class usages, combined with the Christian core to form 'Western civilisation'.

The fact that, for the past half-century or so, those rules have been largely replaced points to something similar to the Constantinian action having occurred in the West around the middle of the twentieth century. We can see the political run-up to it beginning in the early 1930s. The American president, Franklin D. Roosevelt and his advisers decided that, to tackle the economic distress caused by the Depression, a great increase of the federal or central power was required. The resulting policies set in motion a continuing growth of that power which had two culminations: first, in 1945, the acquisition of the atomic bomb and the putting into production of atomic and, later, hydrogen bombs; second, the great financial empowerment of the 1960s that was generated by the cluster of spending 'revolutions', from Vancouver to Vienna, that launched consumerism. Thereafter the growth of American power became self-generating. It was no longer merely state power, but rather, as Tom Wolfe calls it in *The Bonfire of the Vanities,* 'the Power', simply: a hybrid power made up of interlocking government, mass media, science, finance, commerce, the judiciary, and police and military agencies.

In that rise to superpower and beyond, the American rulers chose as doctrinal aides the self-styled 'liberals' of 1930s vintage. Or rather, as in a Communist system, there was a symbiosis: the liberals functioned both as privileged public preachers and as activists in the expanding apparatus of power. The fundamentalist wing of historical Liberalism, they were influential in the Democratic Party. Emerging from the margins to the centre, they gradually replaced the Protestant and Liberal preachers who until then had collaborated with the rulers in determining the rules the nation subscribed to. Their pulpits – few at first, later many – were supplied by the mass media, which included Hollywood films. They increased greatly in number, reach and impact with the arrival of television.

The liberals were utopian idealists who dreamt of a new, clean, bright America, rid of the remaining oppressions of its European heritage: an unhistorical, just society of really sovereign and equal individuals that would live by a better morality than the Christian-Liberal one and, as a society, worship no God. From the European perspective, they were socialists, and, indeed, in the personal histories of many of them there was a shifting overlap with the American Communist Party. The chief agent of the better morality they advocated would be a 'Big State' – as the current phrase went – based on democracy and inspired by their social vision. It would liberate individuals into equal status and active autonomy based on mutual respect.

That was their most obvious coincidence of interest with the ambitious rulers in Washington. But their passion for a secular Power that would liberate individuals contained, implicitly, another common interest of equal importance. It implied the dissolution of any traditional authority – that of old people, clergy, schoolteachers, men, parents, local communities – which, by subordinating individuals, impeded the Big State in its task of liberating them. Clearly, rulers equipped with the necessary means can impose their will more effectively when such dissolution has occurred; when the people they rule have been rendered a mass of individuals, with no intermediate authorities or social adhesions intervening.

From the start, then, in this implicit threat to traditional authority, there was a threat to the inherited rules of Western civilisation that were subscribed to in the USA, as in the European democracies. (Those rules had already been rejected, in some key respects, in the Soviet Union and Nazi Germany.) The threat was sharpened by the fact that the liberals set no limit to the equality and self-rule due to individuals, and none either to the magnification of the liberating ruling power. In both instances, provided democracy was maintained and liberation always the end in view, the more the better. So when the liberating American power, as a result of its atomic incinerations of many Japanese dads and moms and kids, became a superpower, the liberals' reaction was logical. They joined with the rulers in approving those indiscriminate massacres. More decisively, they joined with them in replacing the West's well-known rule on this ethical fundamental by a new, permissive rule.

This quasi-papal act was acquiesced in by the rulers of Western Europe. That, combined with the fact of American superpower and its dominance of the West, opened the way for a general American rule-changing role from Los Angeles to Venice. This role became operative in the 1960s and 70s when, on both sides of the Atlantic, liberal campaigns aimed at general rule-changing got under way. In Western Europe it was, in a sense, a matter of balancing what was already the case in the Soviet satellites where, as the result of measures taken by indigenous Communists, Communist rules were in force. In America's European dependencies, rulers, businessmen and local liberal preachers combined to establish liberal rules.

Concretely, the purpose of these campaigns was dual. They aimed, on the one hand, to invalidate the traditional authorities mentioned above, on the other, to liberate individuals by making them equal, self-determining and mutually respecting consumers of all kinds of goods and sex. The governments contributed by replacing old laws and financial arrangements that supported Christian morality and Western usage by new laws and financial arrangements that accorded with liberal teaching. The ability to acquire things, and the avidity to do so, which the consumerist campaigns released, produced high tax yields that helped to finance the growing stockpiles of nuclear weapons, the new space technology and, in particular, the American race to the moon.

People got progressively richer, were physically healthier, lived longer, and had more individual legal rights than any human beings before them. For the good of the citizens in a

variety of respects, and to boost and guide the growing
economy, the nation-states, flanked by liberal preachers and
experts and commercial advertisers, directed people's
behaviour down to the most private details. They did so
through a combination of legal regulation, ethical injunction,
expert advice and persistent exhortation, all transmitted to the
citizens through the mass media. Colour television brought this
hybrid directive Power forcefully into living-rooms and
kitchens.[4] At the same time, for the citizens' security, states and
larger cities greatly increased their police forces and their
technological surveillance of people's movements and
communications. This series of measures had an inherent logic:
in societies where there has been a great empowerment of the
individuals, social stability requires a proportionate increase in
collective control.

The new rules, as it turned out, were only in part reversals
of old Western rules. Along with permissions and injunctions
in that vein, they included new, liberal 'sins' and virtues. The
former ranged from racism, careless eating and sexual
molestation to smoking and doubting the Holocaust Story. The
virtues included, apart from avoidance of the 'sins', care for the
environment, diligent consumption, and tolerance of abortion,
pornography, and weapons of massacre (if subject to approved
control).[5]

4. It is interesting to notice (see the quotation above from Naomi
Wolf) how the Wolf family in San Francisco became aware of
the change of rules: 'while we watched TV'.

5. These matters are more fully dealt with in my *The Postwestern
Condition: Between Chaos and Civilisation*, London, 1999 (out
of print but available in public and other libraries). Also, in
reconsidered form, in *The Revision of European History,* Ch.10,
'The Dream of Post-Europe', to be published soon by Athol
Books, Belfast (www.atholbooks.com). For some relevant
personal background see *The Turning Point: My Sweden Year
and After,* Sanas Press, 2002 (distributed to bookshops by
Veritas).

In the United States in recent times the liberals have experienced a downturn of fortune. Because the voters, there as elsewhere, have been converging on the political 'centre', professed liberals have lost favour in the Democratic Party where previously they were at home. Considered too 'left', they are often an electoral liability. But the new order that they and their European colleagues helped to put in place between the 1940s and the 1970s remains in place. And both in the US and in Europe, many people who would never think of themselves as liberals accept the liberal values and rules as given.

## Christians and the change of rules

In many Western countries before the change of rules – in particular, in Continental Europe – the rulers, as well as large numbers of citizens, had distanced themselves from the Christian churches. In that sense, there was already in the West a partial, so to speak, theological reversal of the Constantinian decision of the years 313 and following. It was partial because those same rulers and citizens continued broadly to support the Christian moral rules as conventions of civil society and international law. They supported them, that is, as norms of 'Western civilisation'. What has now happened, with the general overthrow of that rules system, is that the reversal of the Constantinian decision has become complete. In the Western empire as a whole, and in its constituent nation-states, the rulers, whatever their personal convictions, are now fully committed to a post-Christian course and endorse preachers who spell out that course, generally and in detail.

Not only is this fact of importance to Christians; equally important is their understanding that it is so and that it has implications for the foreseeable future. The rulers of the West no longer regard the Christian preachers, whether as purveyors of theology or of morality, as a useful adjunct to their rule and power. On the contrary, they regard them as a threat to this; and because the Catholic Church is the main embodiment of

Christian preaching, they regard it, in that role – it can still be useful in some social-service roles – as a particular thorn in their side.

Their antagonism to it is well-founded. The first rule proclaimed by Catholic preaching is that individuals and nations must worship God and, as part of that worship, obey His law. And that 'law', spelt out as rules, is fundamentally at variance with the established rules on which the power and prosperity of the West – as a whole, and in its constituent nation-states – depend. This means that from Los Angeles to Warsaw and beyond, committed Catholics and other Christians find themselves for the foreseeable future in a situation not unlike that of their antecedents in the Roman Empire before Constantine. Or, to put it in another, illuminating way, in the West the Church now finds itself in something like the situation which has been normal for it throughout the world since it first emerged as an international community. The case of Europe, at home and overseas, was quite exceptional. Something like it may be repeated in the future, say, for example, in China; but the Christian West, though Islam has not yet fully realised this, is now, in all likelihood, an episode of past history.

The Church must, by its very nature, reject the West's new rules of behaviour as a 'package' for human beings to live by. Their basic premise is that God is unnecessary for a good human life. A number of them are fundamentally at variance with the Christian moral rules. Collectively, moreover, because they are chaotic – because they have not been ordered into the sense-giving hierarchy that a civilisation requires – they deliver to whomever looks to them for sense in life, a sock on the jaw. The Church is the sworn opponent of senselessness. But at the same time, the Church, sifting through the liberal rules, finds some of them quite acceptable. Some of them have even inspired the Church to rethink and refine certain elements of its moral teaching. On any pilgrimage, let alone a pilgrimage through history, one meets interesting people, including some who are hostile but who say things worth heeding.

## Fundamentalist liberalism in Ireland

In Ireland, more specifically in the Republic, the change to the new rules was not a matter of our rulers taking a sovereign and shrewd decision in the interests of their sovereign power. Just as imperative word went out in the Soviet sphere, say, in Romania or Bulgaria, that a regime change was called for, so, too, in the American sphere, of which the Republic was a minor unit. It was a matter of survival, given the imperial structure of the West.

Insofar as the liberal rule-changes were of a peripheral nature, the Irish accepted them readily, without a thought. But the campaign by Irish liberals to change the rules on central moral issues took longer than elsewhere. And even now, though it has managed to make many Catholic women self-permissive on abortion, it has still failed to bring about a clear, democratically supported rule-change. The reason for this hard slog on central matters, as compared with other parts of the West, was that our liberals were up against a more difficult situation than that which usually faced their colleagues. For most of those colleagues most of the time, it was a matter of overthrowing rules which for many or most of the citizens were a mere matter of civil convention. In Ireland, for almost everyone, including the rulers, the rules governing the central moral matters were *religious rules* anchored in faith; corollaries of Catholic worship; even distinguishing and bonding symbols of nationality. So the Irish liberals had a dual task. They had to combine their persuasive arguments in favour of the new rules as such, with propaganda directed to breaking the bonds of faith, worship and nationality that attached Irish Catholics to their Church and in particular to its clergy. In this last respect, in recent years, the revelations relating to some Catholic-run industrial schools, and the clerical 'sex scandals', were gifts to them which they used to the hilt.

Irish fundamentalist liberalism was not always openly anti-Catholic. Given the special difficulties of the Irish situation, it had at first to tread softly. As preached by the *Irish Times* and the nascent Telefís Éireann in the years of the Second Vatican Council, it took, with regard to religion, a soft form. It was directed merely against bad 'conservative, puritanical' *Irish* Catholicism, as opposed to the good 'liberal' Catholicism that was being proclaimed by the Council and that supposedly reflected Catholicism 'on the Continent'. And even when, in the course of the 70s, it assumed an increasingly anti-Catholic form, Catholicism was not its sole target. From the start, in the 1960s, our liberals had also been 'revisionists' with regard to Irish nationalism, past and present.

Generally speaking, it was in the 70s that Irish liberalism moved from soft to hard. Talk was first heard then of the 'liberal agenda'. The Irish Press and Independent newspapers, and the Dublin secular magazines, became, in the colourful Nazi expression, *gleichgeschaltet* (brought into line). They conformed to the *Irish Times*-RTÉ axis. A similar development occurred among the politicians. The 60s saw the incipiently liberal initiatives of Seán Lemass on the economy, the North and the Irish language, and George Colley's commission on the Constitution, established with a view to revising it. Then, from the 70s onwards, there followed the at first reluctant, later resigned collaboration of the political class with the liberal programme of fundamental rule-changing.

As the repeated liberal attacks on the Constitution soon made clear, our fundamentalist liberals were opposed to the amalgam of values which it represented. These comprised worship of the Christian God; the classical or 'Victorian' Liberalism which had been the secular creed of Irish Catholics since Daniel O'Connell's time; the liberationist nationalism which, in Ireland as in other foreign-dominated European nations, was an intrinsic part of that Liberalism; and elements of Catholic morality and social teaching. Insofar as the worldview, rules and norms derived from that amalgam clashed with fundamentalist liberal orthodoxy, as transmitted by London, our liberals wanted to replace them with that orthodoxy neat.

The anti-nationalist and ultimately anti-national strain of Irish liberalism is clearly not a standard component of the liberal or consumerist ideology. It is not to be found in other Western nations. The explanation for it seems to lie in a combination of two factors. First, the fact that liberalism emerged in Dublin mainly as an import from London awakened atavistic colonised sentiments in the Irishmen involved. Second, inasmuch as the historical bond of Catholicism with the nation and its liberation struggle strengthened the Church, that struggle and the nation it struggled for had to be invalidated. In this vein, the Easter Rising and what led to it and flowed from it was a compound of immoral violence and bigotry.[6] The Irish nation included an important non-Catholic, non-nationalist element which must – so the argument went – have a determining role in its rules and ethos. First, until contrary evidence made the notion clearly ridiculous, that determining component of the nation was the Ulster British; then, in more recent years, the thousands of immigrants from a variety of races and cultures. When the liberal animus against nationalism and the historical nation formed a common front with the explicit anti-Catholicism, the net result was antagonism to the reality and the very notion of a distinctive

---

6.   Naturally, within liberalism, there were shadings and divergences between 'card-carrying' and *à la carte*. Garret FitzGerald, a notable liberal, has argued that the Easter Rising was justified because it led to the establishment of an independent Irish state and thus made possible Irish membership of the European Union.

personality of Ireland. Implied was the suggestion that Ireland's only legitimate existence is as a somewhat differently coloured extension of England – or of England and the USA combined. In this respect, Irish liberalism has been aimed at substantially defeating the purpose of the Irish Revolution. In that purpose, a separate Irish state occupied a merely facilitating role for nation-building in line with the nation's historical heritage.

The Irish Catholic Church was never a state church. But it was for centuries, until not long ago, both in tacit understanding and in concrete fact, the Church of the Irish nation. Almost all those who considered themselves members of that nation were active church members. For the most part – there were significant exceptions – the nation's political leaders and leaders of opinion belonged to it. The political leaders, moreover, whether Catholic or not, were normally at pains to have the Church's moral approval; and they endorsed its role as teacher of the nation from Derry to Cork. The Church enjoyed, in other words, the substance, if not the legal form, of the Constantinian arrangement.

That situation has changed fundamentally. The Church is no longer, in the senses just mentioned, the Church of the Irish nation. It is a matter for debate in what proportions this is due to the success of liberal preaching and propaganda in alienating people from the Church; the Church leadership's neglect of due moral housekeeping with regard to deviant clergy and religious; and, during the decades of the Northern war, the same leadership's greater identification with the policies of the Irish and British states than with the Catholic people and their nation.[7] All three have been contributory

---

7.   Compare, by contrast, the joint pastoral letter of the Irish Catholic bishops in 1920, during the War of Independence. In how many parishes, and how often, in the years 1969-85, were prayers led from the altar for 'our suffering brothers and sisters in the North'? Living in Conamara and Dublin I never experienced it.

factors. But the decisive reason why the Catholic Church is no longer the Church of the Irish nation is that there is no longer any such nation for it to relate to. More precisely, the Irish nation which achieved a second historical incarnation between, roughly, 1790 and 1845 has ceased to exist. It consisted of the Irish Catholic people, their Church and their non-Catholic Irish allies, engaged together in a freedom struggle aimed at national restoration. Its Catholicism and its freedom struggle, so understood, were in fact, and in the eyes of the world, its main distinguishing, bonding and defining features. The disclaimer of those distinguishing bonds by its political and ideological leadership of recent decades has dissolved it. Now, in a sort of subconscious declaration of its present condition, the ghost nation has chosen out of 1500 years of national history, as the principal monument of its capital city, a tall, mute, steel Spike, such as might more suitably distinguish the other Blackpool.

This, of course, is merely to describe the situation as it is. It is not to speculate on a possible future reincarnation of the nation nor of the Church's possible role in that.

## The mass media

Many words have been wasted discussing 'why the media are critical of the Church' (leave aside 'opposed to it'). Mainly such talk is about the mass media's notion of 'news values' and the allegedly critical inclination of journalists generally. That the latter is nonsense is evidenced by the Dublin media's ability to be uncritical, adulatory and protective with regard to their chosen heroes or favoured groups. But the fact is that 'the mass media' are not by their nature critical of Christianity or the Church. In the twentieth century up to the 1950s, in Britain and the USA, quality newspapers were generally supportive of Christian values and rules, respectful towards Protestant churches, and objective towards the Catholic Church. Until half a century ago, in the Republic of Ireland and in the nationalist North, the press in general was reverential towards the Catholic

Church; and the *Irish Times*, though not 'pro-Catholic', usually took care not to offend Catholics. If the West's mass media, generally, are now unsupportive of Christianity, and openly opposed to many of its values and rules, that is because the general regime has changed in the manner I have been describing, and the media speak for it.

Vincent Twomey, in *The End of Irish Catholicism?*, writes: 'It is incontestable that, from the point of view of the Catholic Church, the Irish media can be described as the most hostile media in the developed world.' Twomey cannot have in mind most of the provincial press, including the Northern nationalist papers. He is presumably referring mainly to the mass media that have national reach – the Dublin media in particular – and if so, what he says is incontestable. Irish quality newspapers have occasionally lowered themselves to the level of Paisleyite rags. Bigotry poses as liberalism. An RTÉ radio interview with a Catholic priest can, as Twomey says, seem like 'an interrogation by the thought-police'. Often, instead of the respect called for by good manners when one is discussing religious matters with someone whose faith one doesn't share, there is boorishness.

Granted, when a new band of preachers is struggling to replace another that has long been firmly in the saddle, the new men will naturally express hostility to their predecessors. The early Christian clergy in Ireland were probably not nice to the druids. But the extreme hostility and nastiness of Dublin liberals, which foreign visitors remark on, begs explanation. It seems to me to arise from three factors. The anti-Catholic journalists and others feel that they must strike hard because, after thirty years of persuasive effort, they are still up against strong Catholic allegiance and sentiment among the people. (Recall the special difficulty of the Irish situation referred to above.) Again, most of them, having had a Catholic upbringing, are converts to anti-Catholicism and are filled with the well-known zeal of converts. Finally, we see at work here the common Irish inclination to 'provincial exaggeration'.

This trait, which is to be found in all provinces, first struck me, in a trivial form, when the 'daring' mini-skirt was introduced all those years ago. In Paris, girls wore it only if they believed it suited their figure, but in Mayo (I happened to travel through it) every girl was wearing one. It struck me again – and I was not the only one – a few years ago, when the new Irish law on homosexual practice made the age of consent lower than in Britain. Consider, too, the universal take-over in the Republic of 'Ms.' instead of 'Miss', while in London some used the ugly and mispelt Americanism, and others, exercising their good taste, didn't. Vincent Twomey remarks on – a much weightier matter – the similarly immoderate and unthought-through acceptance in Ireland of the liturgical reforms of the Second Vatican Council. Underlying provincial exaggeration is a desperate desire, for reasons of self-esteem, to display conformity – which is often actually an imagined conformity – with the power centres, and to feel approved of by them.

Doubtless this same compulsion is at work in our ruling elite's exaggerated interpretation of 'separation of Church and State', which they convert into separation of religion from the public sphere. By European standards, their secularist zeal would be comical if it were not so sad – and impoverishing.[8] It is reflected in the scarcity of Christian feastdays which are also Irish public holidays and the refusal to correct this when, some years ago, by an edict of the European Union, the Republic was required to increase its number of public holidays. Notoriously it was reflected in the refusal to allow the weekly *Irish Catholic* to advertise on radio, and later – after a legal amendment – in

---

8. Filtered down to local level in towns, rural districts and city parishes and suburbs, this sadly fanatical 'secularism' greatly impoverishes Irish culture and takes from foreign tourism in Ireland. We know this. In many parts of Europe, when we travel, we are spectators at beautiful or striking public religious celebrations organised by municipal authorities in collaboration with the Church.

the permission for it to do so if it didn't claim the Catholic Church does good! And yet again, it has cropped up in the technical and other difficulties that have been put in the way of a Christian radio station.

I speak for more than myself when I say that the emergence of a powerful band of anti-Catholics among the Irish Catholic people hurts me personally; and this for reasons connected not with ideology or religion but with brotherliness and solidarity. We have come through long hard times together, we Irish Catholic people, times when we were not only oppressed politically and socially, but had our religion mocked and for a time actually persecuted. During those centuries we developed, males and females, a sense of fellowship, a predisposition of friendliness towards each other even on first encounters, which survived into the better times of the twentieth century. Our deepest, usually unspoken bond, was our awareness that we were Catholics together, whether good or bad, in a non-Catholic environment, and that being Catholic was part of our nationhood – even if mere adherence to Ireland also sufficed for inclusion in that. The pain of this solidarity ending is intensified by the emergence among us of a band whose speech and behaviour are reminiscent of those of our historical enemies.

Not sufficiently understood by Irish Catholics is the reason why the statement 'the national mass media are anti-Catholic' can be made with truth. The reason is that Ireland has no Catholic mass media – something which, like the paucity of religious public holidays, would also cause surprise in Continental Europe, not to mention Muslim countries. A visit to any Irish newsagent's, even large ones, confirms, with regard to print media, this remarkable fact. (The *Irish Catholic* sells its 27,000 weekly copies almost entirely inside churches or through private distributors. The Irish-language weekly, *Foinse*, directed at a much smaller readership, is available in most newsagent's.)

More than 170 years after Catholic Emancipation, there is no Irish Catholic journal like the English *Tablet*, selling throughout the English-speaking world and beyond it, mainly in lands that the Irish Church has actively evangelised. In Ireland there is no Catholic radio station, not even a pirate one. (In Conamara, in the early 1970s, we set up a pirate Gaeltacht station, which later evolved into Raidió na Gaeltachta.) Nor is there any Catholic television, even a local station. (Again, in Conamara, an impromptu local television preceded the setting up of TG4. In Najaf, the Shiite holy city in Iraq, three weeks after the overthrow of Saddam Hussein's government, a local television was broadcasting Shiite good news.)

Even more remarkable is the fact that the absence of pro-Catholic mass media has continued in the face of the increasing anti-Catholicism of the national media. Éamon de Valera, in the 1930s, faced with a similar situation with regard to Fianna Fáil, set up the daily *Irish Press* to remedy the matter. Money cannot be the problem for the Catholic Church, which has shown its ability to raise vast sums to cater to physical hunger in Ethiopia and elsewhere. One way or another, and whatever the reason, the absence of Catholic mass media is an important factor conditioning – and obstructing – the preaching of the Gospel in Ireland.

When to this public silence is added the decisions to end Corpus Christi and May processions, and to abolish Lenten fasting – once the subject of much good-humoured Catholic and non-Catholic banter – a strange thought emerges. Does the Irish Church believe that being publicly inaudible and imperceptible is an effective way of making Christ present in Ireland and of winning followers for him in our four green fields? Or is it simply carelessness?

## Democracy and pluralism

Western democracy defines itself as being, among other things, pluralist. It distinguishes itself, in this respect, from totalitarian and one-party regimes. Democratic pluralism is based on the premise that a society contains diverse worldviews and cultures and that this plurality is entitled to institutional representation. It derives from constitutional rights to freedom of expression, association and religion. Pluralism entails the recognised existence, within an agreed constitutional framework, of diverse ideological or religious groups and, on occasion, linguistic or ethnic groups. When such groups are represented by recognised political parties, this constitutes 'political pluralism'. Its corollary is a similarly representative pluralism in the mass media. However, since the 1960s, and even more since the fall of Communism, a number of factors have combined to virtually annul such pluralism in fact.

In each nation-state there has been a convergence of the principal parties – including those which have 'Christian' in their names – towards an ideologically 'central' position. 'Left' and 'Right', though still brandished because habits die hard, have become tattered coats which no longer enclose substantial, contrasting bodies. The new, all-conquering 'central' position is based on an amalgam of liberal ethics and 'neo-liberal' economics that furthers consumption. As a result of winning out in all the nation-states, it has become the prevailing ideology in the West; the ideology of the Western empire. Within its limits, variations are possible, but only to the degree that they were possible and occurred in successive Communist governments of the Soviet Union, and as they occur, over time, in the policies of any one-party state.

The net result, if we except small parties representing extreme positions which have no chance of prevailing, is that 'political pluralism' has shrunk to being a merely nominal thing. It is a matter of political factions representing different emphases and slants within a common framework of mentality and purpose. Regardless, therefore, of electoral outcomes, effectively the same government is always in power. Inevitably, this decay of political pluralism, in the party sense, has been accompanied by a parallel decay of mass-media pluralism. Shadings and slants apart, there has been an ideological convergence of the secular mass media under the homogenising pressure of television. The overall effect has been a corruption of Western democracy in the direction of a 'soft' ideological totalitarianism: that is, a state of affairs in which a single ideology is imposed by legislation derived from it and by overwhelming persuasion, while dissident views are accorded some publicity and defined as wrong.

The Italian writer, Claudio Magris, best known for his book *The Danube*, commented in 1997 on the significance and effect of the 'overwhelming persuasion'. In a book of essays he wrote:

> The defeat of political totalitarianism in many countries... does not preclude the possible victory of a 'soft' and colloidal totalitarianism capable of inducing the masses to believe that they want what their rulers consider appropriate.[9]

Things have progressed in that direction since 1997.

Leave aside the rise of Islam in the West and what that may come to signify. A side-effect of the homogenisation just described is that the Catholic Church, and those Protestant churches which are least willing to compromise with the prevailing ethos, have willy-nilly acquired a unique political role. They have become the main reason why Western democracy can still lay claim to being pluralist and not, in ideological terms, quasi-totalitarian. And that, in turn, is the fundamental reason why the anti-pluralist dynamic of liberal consumerism is intent on eroding them.

---

9.    'In Attesa del Destino' in *Dialoghi in Cattedrale*, Rome, Edizioni San Paolo, 1997.

In the microcosm of the Republic of Ireland we have seen those overall processes reproduced. Within living memory, Fianna Fáil, Fine Gael and Labour spoke for ideologically diverse sections of the electorate. The *Press* and *Independent* newspapers and the *Irish Times* put forward different ideological viewpoints and Radio Éireann was neutral on public issues. So, too, except on Vatican Council issues, was the new television station in the 1960s. Oddly, during the decades which saw such pluralism come to an end, our liberals – a small band at first, then increasingly more – were arguing that the main aim of their agenda was to make the Republic a 'pluralist society'! Along with the pluralist phenomena just referred to, the remarkable pluralism of our schools system and our state-promoted linguistic pluralism made nonsense of their pretension. What they in fact hoped for – and showed by treating non-liberal views with contempt – was the increasing ideological monism that their missionary zeal has in fact produced. 'Adherence by everyone' is, after all, what every ideological grouping, including the Church, is out to achieve.

The first step towards achieving that in a constitutionally pluralist democracy is to bring about ideological monism in its representative agencies – the political parties and the mass-media organs. This monism was displayed, in extreme form, by our Soviet-style referendums of the past twenty years. Repeatedly, on matters of great national importance, all the main political parties, the national print media, and RTÉ by its obvious bias, spoke for the same side on the question at issue. The half to one third of the voters who still managed to think differently were indeed free to advertise their dissidence by ad hoc ways and means; but they were virtually unrepresented by the representative agencies that the democracy had provided.

Granted, those referendums were extreme instances of the representative quasi-monism achieved; but they were that only inasmuch as they brought crudely into the open the everyday perversion of our democracy's representative system. Contrary to the implication if not the letter of the Republic's Constitution, that system has ceased to represent, anything like adequately, the plurality of value systems and convictions which Irish society contains. Inasmuch as this offends against the implicit meaning of the Constitution agreed by the people, it is an injustice which they, as Sovereign, are committing, actively and passively, against themselves.

It is an injustice which affects, among others, the Catholic citizens, clergy and laity, as members of the Catholic Church. The Republic's representative system does not include anything like due representation of their value system and convictions. That is true, but it is also true that, given their large numbers and their civil rights in a nominally pluralist democracy, their efforts to right this injustice have not been correspondingly energetic or efficacious. Apart from a couple of faltering attempts to create a Catholic political party – faltering because a confessional party is not part of our tradition – these have been confined to ad hoc mobilisations by laypeople to contest a referendum or a proposed law. Granted, such ad hoc efforts were intended to influence the behaviour not only of voters, but also of Dáil deputies, with regard to the particular matter at issue. But they did not amount to efforts to remedy the unjust representative system permanently; and even on their own terms, as ad hoc agitation, they did not include the massive street demonstrations which Catholics, clergy and laity together, could have organised.

Take the case of RTÉ, which is legally bound to reflect the nation's culture. In fact, and in the eyes of the world, Catholicism has always been and remains a central element of Irish culture. For RTÉ to have fulfilled, during the years of its existence, its legal obligation with regard to this fact, it would have needed to programme very differently than has been its practice. It would not have relegated Catholicism to a sector of a woolly 'Religious Affairs Department'. It would have presented films, documentaries, soaps and devotional events of

Catholic interest as a substantial part of its mainstream programming on either or both of its channels.[10] The traditional-music lobby and the GAA, dissatisfied with the treatment they were being accorded by RTÉ, took effective measures to get this remedied by the national broadcaster. Gaeltacht activists and the Irish-language lobby expressed their dissatisfaction with the space given to Irish on RTÉ by taking effective measures to get Irish-language radio and television services with state support. The Catholic people, clergy and laity, scarcely aware, it would seem, of the disregard with which they were being treated, did nothing in particular to remedy the situation. (Not only in this regard, but in others of a similar nature, several interesting test cases have not been taken to the High Court.)

What is the reason for the relatively weak response of Catholics to their inadequate public representation in recent decades? In an immediate sense, it lies in our collective failure to conceive of ourselves in civic terms, as a group with rights of adequate representation in a constitutionally pluralist democracy. This seems to have been particularly the case with regard to our bishops, clergy and religious – that is to say, our leadership. Collectively, these leaders seem to have had an inadequate consciousness of themselves as citizens entitled, first, to express their convictions opportunely and

10. Apart from this being a due fulfilment of its public-service obligation, it would have made commercial sense. RTÉ would have been supplying a large Irish audience with a much-appreciated service which they could not get from any of the competing British channels. Even late in the day, the two million people who turned out to honour the remains of St Thérèse on their journey through Ireland might have suggested this to RTÉ's managers. But ideologically blinkered to the Irish reality, they opted, instead, to plead their dire financial state and to ask for another rise in the licence fee. Now, six months after getting that, they are back where their blinkers have put them and asking for more of the spurious remedy that has repeatedly failed.

inopportunely; second, to mobilise their followers in the demand that those convictions be publicly heard. Oddly, this does not seem to have been the case a century and more ago, under British rule. But because bishops, clergy and religious, male and female, do still constitute the Catholic leadership, their faltering civic consciousness has been the main immediate factor impeding the growth of such consciousness in Catholics generally.

However, the lack in question, whether in leadership or laity, seems, in turn, to be caused by another factor. Mention there of how things were rather different under British rule suggests it. In the Republic, in particular, we Catholics have not clearly recognised that this republic, which we once assumed, with well-founded confidence, was 'ours', both as Irish and as Catholics, is no longer that in the latter sense. Rather than being, in a moral sense, owners of the republic, we have become, as Irish Catholics, a religious body that lives in it, and that is out of favour with its rulers and endorsed preachers. From having been for us, as Irish and as Catholics, 'our home' in the world, it has now become for us, as Catholics, a state in which we must create and defend a home. Obviously, our inadequate consciousness that this change has occurred, and that things are now that way, has prevented us from drawing the necessary conclusions of a civic, political and defensive nature. Should our consciousness develop to match the situation, Catholics in the Republic may find that the Church north of the border has some useful things to teach them.

Especially when it has to do with worldviews, effective pluralism is a benefit to a society because it sharpens minds. The intellectual slackness that has befallen Continental countries since the fall of Communism makes this point. Obviously, the Catholic Church has more to offer Irish society than a sharpening of minds: it offers, as well as that, food for the spirit and soul, a humanising ethic, and a present and everlasting life with God. It follows that, when our pluralist democracy is failing to represent this offering, to a just degree, in its political system and its mass media, the Church has a civic duty, as well as a Christian obligation, to remedy this insofar as it can. How thrillingly this can be done, even by a small group of Catholics, has been evidenced, in a variety of media, by the monks of Glenstal. 'Thrillingly' because of its quality of joyous counterattack agaíntt the materialistic monism threatening Ireland.[11] But how little has been done in this regard is evidenced by the absence from that threatening monism of – so many things, but a few will do:

- the Rosary broadcast on a drive-home programme at evening rush hour as the traffic snakes bumper to bumper;
- a corner in video shops marked 'Religion' that contains the films and documentaries of Catholic interest that RTÉ very rarely broadcasts;
- a Saturday column in a newspaper, available in every newsagent's, which explains the historical context and theological thrust of the (otherwise often baffling) Sunday Mass readings;
- at 3 a.m. on an all-night radio for the sleepless, Christ's discourse to the Apostles at the Last Supper from St John's Gospel;
- a Church-sponsored campaign, from altar steps, by leafleting and by street demonstrations, urging the Government to lead and assist in a concerted national effort to reduce suicides and abortions by five per cent a year.

Absences such as these impede the preaching of the Gospel in Ireland.

---

11.     Although it has had less public resonance, the much-used Jesuit website 'Sacred Spaces' deserves mention in this context.

## Modernity and the Irish Church

Books about the Celtic Tiger years which suggest that in those
years, for the first time, Ireland entered 'modernity' or
underwent 'modernisation' misrepresent. The same is true of
suggestions that these events have occurred, for the first time,
in the period since the 1960s. Thirty years ago, the historian
Joe Lee, who knows what he is talking about, published a book
called *The Modernisation of Irish Society 1848-1918*.
Speaking broadly, 'modernity' is, and always has been, the
latest thing in vogue in the power centres, which rapidly
spreads to the provinces and is eagerly adopted by the
provincials, led by their elites. In that broad sense, modernity
has existed, and Ireland has been modernising, at least since
the Iron Age. And it will continue to modernise for the
forseeable future.

Be that as it may, historians of Europe have for long given
'modern' a special meaning, as describing the period since
around 1500. Historians of ideas and sociologists have given it
another and narrower special meaning: the social processes
and mentality characteristic of, respectively, the most
advanced Western nations and their progressive classes from
the late 1700s. By general agreement, as an amalgam of these
special meanings, modernity reached its apex in the Victorian
period and lasted until World War II or the 1950s. Regarding
the subsequent period, there has been a divergence of views
among academics and intellectuals generally, with a majority
holding that 'modernity' as such had ended. Some call the
following period 'late modern', others 'postmodern'.[12]

What emerges from this is that there has been no clash
between 'modernity', in its most widely accepted sense, and the
Catholic Church in Ireland. On the contrary, the high period of

---

12.   In my own recent writings I have opted for 'postwestern' or
      'post-European'.

modernity in the West coincided with the greatest flourishing of the Irish Church since the sixth and seventh centuries (it lasted into the 1960s). The men and women who led and shaped the Church in that period were, in the most accepted sense of the term, modern personalities of Christian faith. Their commitment to political Liberalism – the leading European ideology after 1850 – and to democracy put the Irish Church at odds with the contemporary teaching of the papacy on political morality. This commitment also facilitated – as has often been remarked – the accommodation of emigrant Irish Catholics to the political mores of the United States of America.

## Irish exceptionalism

The notion of 'Irish exceptionalism', the idea that the Irish and their habits are 'odd' in an uncivilised or obtuse sense, or amusingly, has been propagated by the English for many centuries. Its basic thrust is to suggest that we Irish diverge in our personalities and our way of doing things from the human norm, or from the norm current in Western societies. Except in trivial respects such as apply to every nation, this has never been true. More specifically, it has never been true that our ways of being or behaving have differed markedly from those of other peoples, Western or non-Western, involved in similar circumstances. But the exceptionalist fiction has survived its lack of truth.

Absorbed through the centuries by the Irish as a belief about themselves, it has had – as our colonisers intended it to have – a debilitating effect. Assisting our assent to it has been our relative geographical isolation, which has deprived us of habitual contact with a variety of peoples and cultures. But believed for one reason or another, the fiction in question has done more than debilitate: it has led to the writing and uttering of a great deal of twaddle about Irish affairs by Irish men and women who are either ignorant of the world beyond southeast

England or unobservant of it. When, as has often been the case in recent years, the exceptionalist fiction is used by such scribblers or wafflers with an intent similar to that of our historical colonisers – namely, to embarrass and weaken us and bend us to their will – it is an ugly spectacle.

## The language environment

From the start, the preaching of the Gospel has adapted to the general and particular language environment. Classic instances of particular adaptation are Christ's sermons to Palestinians familiar with shepherding, fishing and vine-growing, and St Paul's canny address to the Athenian intellectuals. Because I am a professional communicator, and Bishop Comiskey had the name of being a good communicator with the media, I once wrote to him about a case in point. I wrote that, in Dublin, for the previous twenty years, we had been hearing from the media about various liberations from the oppression of the Church that we had attained or that were desirable. As Catholics, I continued, we were vaguely aware that the Church had always been in the liberation business. So why had this theme not been occurring in the homilies and pastoral letters and in articles in Catholic magazines? Not just liberation, but liberation in the context of the consumerist situation – of the appetites and acquisitive zeals, and the trekking around shopping malls on Sunday, that we were being systematically enslaved to? Why not, indeed, as a deliberate, canny manoevre to counter the charge of Catholic oppression, a stressing of Christianity's liberating mission? I doubted, I said, that I was the only member of the Dublin Catholic middle class to feel let down by the Church's silence on this theme; let down by the failure of our bishops and parish clergy to counter in this manner the false charge against the Church, and against us Catholics as putative dupes of it. But whether or not others felt as I did about it, it was objectively a letting down of us. Not only that, but a silence truly amazing, given that the Church actually had the goods to offer; that liberation was supposed to be the essence of what it was about. I forget whether Bishop Comiskey replied; but whether he did or not is not the point I am making.

In recent times, in response to the language usage of various social milieus – mostly marginalised or youthful milieus – there have been presentations of the Church's message in demotic or hip language. These may have their merit; but I am thinking now about the mainstream voice of the Catholic Church in Ireland in the English language. Apart from a Scripture which is a direct or indirect translation from several ancient languages shaped by as many ancient cultures, the key terms of the current Catholic language in English are derivatives from ancient Latin and Greek. Granted that, in order to have continuity and clarity in theological study, a certain rigidity of terminology is required. But in the preaching of the Gospel, this is not the case. A sensible flexibility is called for and is, indeed, a virtue. I am attempting some thought about this.

For example, I look at the word 'redemption' and, apart from knowing it is the good thing that Christ did or does, my mind, as a language man, draws a blank. I gather that, along with the verb 'redeem', it is a term sometimes used today in financial transactions with which I am not familiar – something to do with bonds? But as a word set before me, it does not represent, intelligibly, something that I want. The dictionary comes up with 'ransom'. But I feel no need to be ransomed. I have not been kidnapped. Yes, I do know that 'redemption' refers etymologically, to a transaction described in the Graeco-Roman world as 'buying back', as from captivity or slavery, and that the early Christians used this as a metaphor for what Christ did – or does? (here I would need some theology to help out). But a metaphor is a metaphor, and the early Christians, left free by Christ to define the exact nature of his cosmic action, could just as well have chosen another metaphor that would mean more to me.

To escape from the Latinate – or Graecoid – bind towards a conceptual flexibility that facilitates a linguistic counterpart, it is useful to examine how languages outside the Latin tradition dealt with such terms. In Gaelic usage, *fuascailt* was the word chosen for *redemptio*; in German it was *Erlösung.* Both are words still in variable living use in those languages (the Irish word somewhat more so than the German). Both have a primary meaning of 'deliverance, release, liberation' and therefore can also, by extension, mean 'ransom'. Etymologically, they derive from the former, broad concept, not from any notion involving payment of money; and yet they have worked for many centuries to convey efficiently what Christ did. And an interesting point: the Irish for 'Christ the Redeemer' is, literally, *Críost an Fuascailteoir,* but it sounds foreign to the language. *Fuascailteoir* doesn't seem to have caught on; Irish Christianity (at least as it has reached us) worked without it. *Críost an Slánaitheoir* was made to suffice. Thus, *slánaigh*, which means, very clearly, 'make whole' or 'heal', functioned also, along with *fuascail*, as a rendering of 'redeem'. Notice that the operative notion here is not, as in Greek, Latin or English, 'saving', but 'healing', as also in the German rendering of 'saviour': *Heiland*, from *heilen*, to heal.

Why, I ask myself, since the Second Vatican Council, have they taken to saying – instead of 'say Mass' – 'celebrate the *Eucharist*'? That word used to mean 'host', which meant 'sacred bread' – and sometimes also the wine. In the Greek usage which it came from, it meant 'thanksgiving'. All of which leaves, to put it mildly, a lot to explain. But it also raises this question: is there not a case for treating that unmelodious, alien-sounding word as quite unnecessary outside theology books? 'Come to me all you who are stressed and overworked, and I will refresh you, for my yoke...'. Mentally renovating, I get that far, and am held up by 'yoke' – which apart from referring to a long disused method of haulage, is in Ireland a word of dubious meaning.

I could go on, but others can do that. In these matters there is no reason why the Irish should not be innovative, as they once were. Correction: there is no reason why the Irish shouldn't innovate, full stop.

## The paedophilia scandals

The recent mass-media outcry about clerical paedophilia has occurred only in the three English-speaking countries, Ireland, Britain and the United States. Ten years ago there was a similar media outcry in English-speaking Canada. For the Catholic Church in these countries to understand the phenomenon in question – and obviously, it is important for the Church to understand it – two questions must be researched and answered. Was it the case that there were more paedophile clergy and religious in these countries than in other Western countries, or was it the case that only in these countries did the media make a great deal of commotion about paedophilia of this kind? When that has been answered, and the phenomenon in question duly identified, as X, the second question follows. To what distinguishing, common feature in the culture of these four countries is the phenomenon X to be attributed? It can hardly be simply the English language.

## The foods the Irish need

There can be no doubt that it was of help to Jesus's roving mission when word got around that it was accompanied by an efficient catering service, that free consultations with the Healer were available, and that these were likely to result in a cure. Love directed to people in their temporal needs, as well as a canny instinct for marketing, have always caused the Church to underpin its evangelisation with temporal benefits. Consequently, an adjunct of successful preaching of the Gospel has always been the ability to identify which temporal benefits are most needed, and will be most appreciated, in any given place or circumstance.

Struck, nearly thirty years ago by a role the Church was playing in Poland under the Communist regime, I had an idea. The Polish Church had made its buildings available to the 'alternative scene' in art, literature and thought, that was not approved of by the Communist government. My idea was simply that, in Ireland, a disused monastic or other church building might be made available as a retreat for writers and artists. I wanted a friendly gesture from the Church towards that aspect of Irish culture; a gesture that I thought might redound to the Church's benefit in view of the anti-Church propaganda that was getting under way. (I made the suggestion in appropriate quarters, but nothing came of it.)

Since then, of course, we have acquired a sufficiency of such retreats. That temporal need is no longer there. Indeed, our materially rich country is far from needing or being likely to appreciate a distribution of bread and fish or of their Celtic Tiger equivalents. The dire needs – dire because poorly catered for – are for foods of the spirit and soul.

Our people – amid the debris of their nation, with the inherited Christian rules declared invalid by the Power and no civic ethic to fall back on – are immersed in anomie. Life, appearing senseless, induces much anguish and depression. Attempts, especially by the young and the sensitive, to quench these pains give the Republic one of the highest rates of alcohol consumption and drug abuse in the European Union; drive many young men to suicide; drive many girls to reckless sex and guilty abortions. Talk of 'dire need'; there is a famine of foods for the spirit and soul. I will try to list some of them.

> Silence, in company; being still; thankfulness for existence; the voice of reason and truth; sight of beauty without excitation, simply to contemplate; joy, experienced in the company of others; sight of satisfying coherence and sense in life; joy, experienced walking along a street alone; reverence; music that speaks to the spirit in us; conviction of immortality; a

heartfelt Yes; a shared sense of rootedness in the past and of satisfactory placement in mankind now; the sense of being looked after, come what may; stress and worry lifting and going away; awe – leaving nothing to say, really; a good song sung loudly in unison with others and with knowledge of all the words; thoughtful ease; memory of a festival in which the highpoint was not the drinking; trustful self-disclosure; the feeling of being alright really, despite one's messing – and able to stop messing, with God's help.

* * *

It seems a good point at which to return to Vincent Twomey's programme of 'faith, theology, liturgy, celebration and administrative restructuring', to which what I have written here has been an adjunct. I have produced what I promised: a meditation, which is a very personal thing; and an appetiser, which I hope will leave my readers eager to get on with the meal.

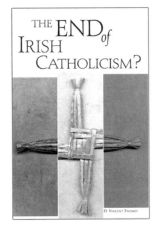

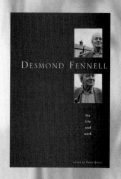
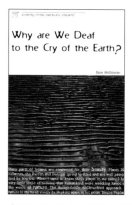
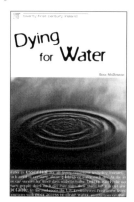